To Dad
Christmas 2007

Lots of love
   from

Danny + Ann
        xxxx

D1492600

The Vulcan Story

The Vulcan Story

Peter R. March

Foreword by
Air Chief Marshal Sir Michael Knight KCB AFC FRAES

Sutton Publishing
in association with the Vulcan to the Sky Trust

Sutton Publishing Limited
Phoenix Mill, Thrupp, Stroud
Gloucestershire, GL5 2BU
in association with the Vulcan to the Sky Trust

First published 2006

British Library Cataloguing in Publication Data
A catalogue for this book is available from the British Library.

ISBN 0-7509-4399-8

Typeset in 9.5/14.5pt Syntax.
Typesetting and origination by
Sutton Publishing Limited.
Printed and bound in England by
J.H. Haynes & Co. Ltd, Sparkford.

CONTENTS

The Vulcan Story is written and published in association with the Vulcan to the Sky Trust (VTST) and will provide support for the VTST education programme. The Trustees of VTST endorse the book and its content.

ALSO IN THIS SERIES

The Concorde Story

The Spitfire Story

I am very grateful for the assistance that I have been given by the Vulcan to the Sky team in the preparation of *The Vulcan Story*. In particular I would like to thank Robert Pleming for his willingness to answer so many questions and for the direct help he gave in checking the text, Felicity Irwin for her support and encouragement and Air Chief Marshal Sir Michael Knight for his Foreword.

I have particularly drawn upon the writing of noted aviation historian Michael J.F. Bowyer and Paul Jackson, Editor of *Jane's All the World's Aircraft*, in researching the Vulcan's development story. In addition I have been helped by Richard Clarkson and Dave Griffiths of the Vulcan Restoration Trust through the excellent publication *Vulcan News*. I am indebted to Brian Strickland for his patient research and collation of information for the narrative and appendices.

As ever it has been a difficult task to select photographs to illustrate the story of this twentieth-century aviation icon from the large number made available by the photographers and collectors who searched their photo files for me. I am particularly grateful to the following: Gordon Bartley, Derek Bower, Michael J.F. Bowyer, Bill Bushell, Sue J. Bushell, Richard Clarkson, Peter J. Cooper, Graham Finch, Jeremy Flack/API, Derek James, Andrew and Daniel March, Robbie Robinson, Kev Storer, Brian Strickland, Charles Toop and Richard L. Ward.

Photo Credits

Photographs Peter R. March/PRM Aviation Collection unless otherwise credited.

FOREWORD

Peter March has produced a very readable summary of the Vulcan's unique place in the story both of the Royal Air Force and of the nation's aeronautical heritage. His work also puts the development of this great aircraft into the context of the fascinating – and genuinely historic – events of the forty-five years that followed the end of the Second World War.

Conceived, built and operated during one of the potentially most dangerous periods of world history, the Vulcan has always served not only as a magnificent and innovative example of British aeronautical design and engineering, but as a most important contributor to the ultimate success of the West's policy of deterrence against war.

That it should have been committed to action only in the very last months of its operational life has a touch of irony about it. However, the lesson of the South Atlantic campaign is that it was brought about as a result of a failure of deterrence – thankfully, at the lower end of the scale of conflict. Happily, the Vulcan proved itself well able to accept the challenge.

This story of a remarkable British aircraft has done much to enthuse the many people who wish to see the last remaining airworthy example of the marque restored to flying condition, and thus once again able to thrill the millions who flock, each year, to air displays across the country. It is with their continued help and support that the vision is becoming a reality.

Air Chief Marshal Sir Michael Knight KCB AFC FRAES
Chairman, Vulcan to the Sky Trust

For forty-five years after the Second World War there was a period of political hostility involving the countries of western Europe and North America, countering the communist threat from the Union of Soviet Socialist Republics (USSR) and Eastern Bloc countries. This 'Cold War' as it is called, dominated international affairs until 1991 and saw many major crises. These included the Berlin Airlift (1948), Korean War (1950), Hungarian uprising (1956), Cuban missile crisis (1962) and the Vietnam War (1965). It was essentially a clash between two different ideologies – Soviet communism and Western capitalism.

Great Britain, the United States and the USSR were allies during the Second World War, but by 1945 the 'friendship' had started to deteriorate. Joseph Stalin, the Soviet leader, distrusted America after President Truman failed to give Russia advance warning of the dropping of the atomic bomb on Japan in August 1945. The signing of the United Nations Charter established the first of the new postwar alliances, as the Soviet Union became increasingly hostile and started to extend its influence across eastern Europe.

British wartime Prime Minister Winston Churchill said in March 1946, 'An Iron Curtain is descending across the continent of Europe.' Communist coups took place in Poland and then Czechoslovakia, leading to the 'Truman Doctrine', whereby President Harry S. Truman urged the USA to 'support free peoples who are resisting attempted subjugation by armed minorities or by outside pressures'.

The first significant postwar test of the West's resolve came in June 1948, with the start of the Soviet blockade of Berlin. Within two days of its imposition, the request from the American Military Governor of Germany for an airlift of supplies was met. The Berlin Airlift became a joint task force of the US Air Forces in Europe, the RAF and civilian operators. Alongside the C-47 Skytrains, C-54 Skymasters and other transports deployed from the USA, there was an increasing number of front-line combat aircraft as the Cold War began to intensify. USAF Strategic Air Command B-29 Superfortresses arrived in Britain in July 1948 and they were soon joined by F-80 Shooting Stars. These jet fighters were deployed to assist the Mustangs and Tempests already providing fighter cover for the airlift, as instances of Soviet fighters 'buzzing' Allied transports flying along the air corridors to Berlin continued.

It was at this time that talks on North Atlantic defence started in Washington. Five nations (Belgium, France, Luxembourg, the Netherlands and the UK) announced the creation of a Western Union Defence Organisation in September 1948. This was a positive move towards firm defensive provision for the region against the growing threat from the USSR.

A few weeks later representatives of these five countries, together with Canada and the USA, announced complete agreement on the principle of a defensive pact for the North Atlantic and on the next steps to be taken. They began the drafting process for the new North Atlantic Treaty and after three months the governments of Denmark, Iceland, Italy, Norway and Portugal also took part. The resulting document was published on 18 March 1949 and the twelve nations signed it on 4 April 1949, establishing the North Atlantic Treaty Organisation (NATO). Key to the alliance's declared defensive purpose was 'that the parties agree that an armed attack against one or more of them in Europe or North America should be considered an attack against them all'.

On 12 May 1949, the Soviet blockade of Berlin came to an end. Even though the situation had eased, the considerably larger military strength of the USSR had not been cut back, unlike the forces of its former allies. Russia held its first atomic A-bomb test on 29 August 1949; the nuclear arms race had commenced. In America the first hydrogen (H-) bomb was exploded in 1952, and in the following year a Russian H-bomb was tested. Although both superpowers built up stocks of nuclear weapons during this period, it was the sheer power of these bombs and the fear that it evoked that prevented a nuclear war, since their use by either side would have inevitably resulted in a catastrophic Third World War. The two superpowers' apparent awareness of each other's capabilities became a deterrent to armed conflict, because of the inherent risk of a

◄
A nuclear explosion is followed by the typical 'mushroom cloud'.

➤

The Titan I and II intercontinental ballistic missiles (ICBMs) were part of the USAF's Cold War nuclear deterrent for a quarter of a century. (via Brian Strickland)

nuclear response – a single bomb was powerful enough to vaporise a whole city.

In the 1950s the US introduced the Boeing B-52 Stratofortress, which could fly 6,000 miles and deliver a substantial nuclear payload. But developments on such a scale required huge financial investment from central government, something which America could afford to do, but which Russia could not. Therefore the Soviets concentrated on building larger bombs and the development of missiles to deliver them. In October 1957 the West was introduced to the fear of a nuclear missile attack, when the Russian *Sputnik* was successfully launched into space. This led to a race for the successful introduction of intercontinental ballistic missiles (ICBMs) and the means of defending against them. The US built the Ballistic Missile Early Warning System (BMEWS) to detect a Soviet missile attack across the Arctic. In the 1960s, the Russians produced more missiles, regardless of quality, whereas the US built fewer, but of better quality.

A British requirement for a revolutionary new bomber came in late 1945. It was spurred on by the development of nuclear weapons, and the need to find a means of quick delivery to deter an aggressor. Possession of such a long-range high-altitude bomber would help with the special Anglo-American relationship, continue to give Great Britain a voice in international affairs and contribute to a Western nuclear deterrent.

The Vulcan's story dates from the 1945 British Air Staff Operational Requirement for a 'state-of-the-art' Avro Lincoln replacement. Refined as Air Staff Requirement B.35/46, issued in January 1947, it called for a bomber with capabilities that would stretch the British aircraft industry's design capacity to a new limit. It specified a multi-engined bomber to replace the Lincoln, capable of carrying a 'special store' (i.e. a nuclear weapon) weighing 10,000lb (4,536kg), or a wide range of conventional weapons of 20,000lb, to a target 1,725 miles (2,780km) away from base. This was to be done at a cruising speed of 575mph (927km/h) from 35,000ft at the beginning of the mission, to 50,000ft after the fuel load had lightened.

A defining factor in the requirement was the size and weight of what would become Britain's first operational atomic bomb – the Blue Danube. The bomb's estimated length was 24ft 2in (7.37m), with a maximum diameter of 5ft (1.52m). Roy Chadwick, the head of the design team, laid down the basic design of the Vulcan in 1947. Tragically killed in an Avro Tudor airliner crash in August that year, he was replaced by William (later Sir William) Farren as technical director, and Stuart Davies, who survived the crash, took over the mantle of chief designer.

Did you know?

The V-bomber specification issued in January 1947 represented more than a 100 per cent advance in speed and altitude performance on the piston-engined Avro Lincoln bomber, then in production for the RAF.

The RAF's new jet bomber had to carry Britain's first operational atomic bomb – the Blue Danube.

because of weight limitations. Instead, pioneering electronic countermeasures, such as jammers, were employed.

The Avro design was for an aircraft with a crew of five, to be carried in a jettisonable capsule, and a maximum weight that would enable it to use existing airfields, after some modification. Meeting all these demands inevitably produced complex, advanced and novel designs. The bomber would need to overfly future missile defences and outperform defending fighters.

Tenders from six contractors were received by 30 April 1947 and, following intensive consideration, Avro was informed on 28 July that its delta design was judged the best. Handley Page's crescent-wing Victor was the runner-up. English Electric did not submit a tender, as it was heavily engaged in getting the Canberra into the air as an interim

The specification also required all-weather capability, high manoeuvrability and provision for radio warning and countermeasures equipment. The provision of defensive tail armament remained a distinct possibility for many years; it was later dropped, but only

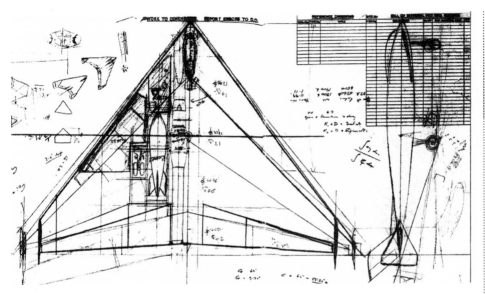

WORK TO DIMENSIONS REPORT ERRORS TO D.O.

A preliminary design sketch for the Type 698 by Roy Chadwick, with workings by Eric Priestley, chief aerodynamicist, shows the outboard vertical surfaces, superimposed engines and offset bomb stowage. (via Vulcan to the Sky)

Lincoln replacement, until B.35/46 designs became available.

Roy Chadwick, Avro's technical director, and Stuart Davis, chief designer, had looked at radical aircraft formats. A possibility was to remove horizontal tail surfaces altogether, thereby saving weight, and design the whole aircraft with a minimal fuselage and large wing. Somehow the span had to be reduced as a weight-saving measure, and thus the

Vulcan was the Roman god of fire and destruction and the name had previously been used by Vickers for a 1920s transport aircraft. The Vulcan's project engineer, Gilbert Whitehead, was not at all impressed by the name. When he looked it up in a mythology book, Vulcan was defined as a 'misshapen god of war thrown out of heaven'.

incorporation of an almost perfect triangle 'delta' wing commenced.

On 27 November 1947, the decision was reached to proceed with the Type 698, Avro's revolutionary four-engined delta-wing design. It featured low wing loading, no high-lift devices, characteristic delta high lift/drag ratio and the potential of reaching a high Mach number.

Because of the Type 698's radical design, it was decided to build a number of one-third deltas to enable additional aspects of the flight characteristics to be explored. This became the Type 707 research aircraft, but the programme was somewhat of an afterthought, as it was run more or less in parallel with its larger relation. However, the 707 programme did provide much valuable research and development data, some of which was applied to the Vulcan – though some say the whole project slowed the Vulcan programme through diversification of effort.

◄
The ill-fated Avro 707 prototype (VX784) here getting airborne for the first time at Boscombe Down on 6 September 1949. Sadly, it crashed less than a month later, killing Flt Lt Esler.
(via Derek James)

◄◄
English Electric produced the twin-jet Canberra light bomber as a stop-gap replacement for the Avro Lincoln.
(Daniel J. March)

9

Flt Lt Eric 'Red' Esler flew the first Avro 707 on 4 September 1949 from Boscombe Down. Flown to Farnborough for static exhibition that month, it crashed near Blackbushe on a test flight on 30 September and Esler was killed. It was thought that, though the aircraft had flown for three hours in total, there had been a control fault which locked the airbrakes open and caused it to stall. No blame was attached to the basic design.

A second aircraft, Avro 707B VX790, that was intended for research into low-speed stability characteristics of delta wings was first flown on 6 September 1950 by 'Roly' Falk. Basically similar to the ill-fated 707, the 707B was also Derwent-powered, but incorporated a wing having 51 degrees of leading-edge sweep-back. It did useful work during the next two years in dispelling many of the myths surrounding delta-winged flight.

Intended for research into the low-speed handling characteristics of delta wings, the Avro 707B VX790 was first flown on 5 September 1950.
(Paul Cullerne/Avro)

In more than 100 hours of research flying it proved an outstandingly docile aircraft.

High-speed data was obtained with a third mini-delta, the Avro 707A WD280, that first flew at Boscombe Down on 14 June 1951. It was designed for operation at the highest possible subsonic speed, and had wing-root intakes, as well as ailerons and elevators, thus making it virtually a one-third-scale model of the Vulcan.

A second 707A, WZ736, made its maiden flight on 20 February 1953, to be used for general research by the RAE. It was also planned to build four side-by-side two-seaters, designated Avro 707C, for RAF delta pilot-training. However, it was soon realised that the Vulcan's flying characteristics did not warrant any special pilot preparation. In the event only one 707C (WZ744) was completed and first flown on 1 July 1953.

➤
Avro's Type 698 was dominated by its huge delta wing and tall fin and rudder.
(via Derek James)

The Avro 698 emerged as an impressive aeroplane, with a wingspan and length just under 100ft (30m), together with a massive wing area of 3,554sq ft (330m^2). Its construction was conventional despite its unusual appearance, most of the aircraft being built from standard high-strength light alloy. In order to save weight some magnesium alloy was included in the bomb doors and control surfaces.

The delta derived its massive strength from the sound structure principles used on the Lancaster, with a two-spar wing of orthodox boom-and-web construction. The centre section was built as a single piece from port to starboard, with cut-outs where appropriate for the engines. Only the crew compartment protruded from the wing.

At first the bomb was to be carried in the wing root, the maximum chord of which was

70ft. Like the Lancaster, the 698 was organised around a very large bomb bay. Operationally very important was the bomber's Mk 1 Navigator and Bombing System, which embraced a navigation computer monitoring ground speed, drift and ground position. This was known as 'NBC' – navigation, bombing, computer.

Two pilots were housed in the cockpit but the three remaining crew members faced rearwards on a lower deck behind the pilots, there being just enough extra room for a visual bombing station in the prone position and two jump-seats in what was only half-jokingly known as the 'coal-hole'. The whole crew compartment caused controversy throughout the Vulcan's career. A jettisonable pressure-cabin capsule was the ideal solution, but very early on, its design proved very difficult to incorporate. The final layout had the two pilots on ejector seats under a small jettisonable canopy incorporating a minimum of window transparencies. The three radio/radar/navigator officers had to exit in an emergency via a shielded door in the floor, then parachute to safety – not an attractive scheme. Many of these 'rear seaters' were unnecessarily lost as a result of the difficulties in escaping from a doomed Vulcan. A total of forty aircrew, including pilots, were killed in twenty-six Vulcan accidents. It should be noted that the Victor bomber, too, had ejector seats only for the pilots.

In the cockpit the pilots had fighter-style stick controls, rather than the usual yoke. An enormous fibreglass radome on the lower half of the nose, covering the radar, was a salient feature, as were the double-bogie Dowty main undercarriage and twin nose wheels. Since the aircraft was a delta, no flaps were fitted.

◀
Cockpit of a later Vulcan, showing its fighter-style controls and its cluttered instrument panel.
(Gordon Bartley)

Did you know?

The Vulcan's weakness was the lack of a reliable escape system for the rear crew. In its original concept, the bomber was to have an ejectable capsule containing all of the crew members, who would remain in their seats and be lowered by a large parachute.

FIRST VULCANS

Manufacture of the prototype Vulcan (VX770) commenced in early 1951, with all but the outer wings built at Avro's main works at Chadderton. The outer wings were built at Woodford, where aircraft were assembled and flight-tested. By the time production of the prototype was under way, it became obvious that the chosen Bristol BE.10 (later named Olympus) turbojet would not be ready in time. Consequently, the decision was taken to install four 6,500lb st (static thrust) (28.9kN) Rolls-Royce RA.3 Avons instead. The second aircraft (VX777) had Bristol Olympus Mk 100 engines, each producing 9,750lb st (43.3kN). Early production Vulcan B1s had yet more powerful

11,000lb st (48.9kN) Olympus 101s. However, this arrangement produced a mild buffeting problem in the outer wings that threatened to eat rapidly into airframe fatigue life. In fact the extra power had allowed them to get to speeds and heights where buffeting was experienced in turns. The answer was the Phase 2 wing with a distinctive kinked leading edge. This new wing was introduced on the sixth production B1.

In August 1952, the first Avro 698 was nearly ready for its maiden flight. A sense

VX770 making a low approach at the Farnborough Air Show, revealing its twin underwing air brakes that were not adopted on production Vulcans. (via Vulcan Memorial Flight)

Much more powerful Bristol Olympus Mk 100 engines, each producing 9,750lb st (43.3kN), were available for the second prototype, VX777.
(Bristol Aeroplane Company)

of competition had developed between the Avro and Handley Page bomber teams to get their aircraft into the air first. In the event Avro won the 'battle' by four months. This was important because it was assumed (albeit incorrectly at the time) that only one of the bombers would be chosen for production, after some kind of competitive evaluation had been carried out.

Shortly before the prototype flew on 30 August 1952, Avro received an order for twenty-five production aircraft, but Handley Page was also contracted to build an initial twenty-five HP.80s. The emerging careers of the 'tin triangle' and its elegant rival was about to begin. By October 1955, eighty-nine Vulcans had been ordered, together with components for a further eighteen.

Handley Page also had an order for twenty-five of the crescent-wing HP.80 Victors.

20

This memorable formation, comprising the second prototype Vulcan (VX777) leading the first (VX770) with four Type 707s, was flown at the Farnborough Air Show in September 1953.
(MAP via Sue Bushell)

Did you know?

RAF Vulcans were painted white as protection against nuclear flash, but when their role was switched to low-level, below-the-radar, attack, the aircraft were painted in grey/green camouflage.

With flight trials going well despite the aircraft's advanced nature, the first production Vulcan B1 made its maiden flight on 4 February 1955. The training unit, No. 230 Operational Conversion Unit (OCU) at RAF Waddington, got its first Vulcan fifty years ago, on 20 July 1956; the first five crews formed the nucleus of No. 83 Squadron on 21 May 1957, also at Waddington.

By the time the forty-fifth and last B1 was delivered, on 30 April 1959, the Mk 104 engine and inflight-refuelling probe were standard, and the designation changed to B1A with the addition of a large ECM (electronic countermeasures) installation in a

Did you know?

The RAF paid about £750,000 for each of the early production Vulcans.

In return it received 167,063 separate parts (excluding engines), 410,300 nuts, bolts, washers and rivets, and approximately 2 miles (3km) of tubing, together with 14 miles (22.5km) of electrical wiring.

The first production Vulcan B1 (XA889), used for development flying, shows the modified wing with its kinked leading edge.
(via Derek James)

XA893, the fifth
production Vulcan B1,
seen here at Moreton
Valence for under-
carriage tests with Dowty.
The first production
Vulcans were painted
overall silver.
(via Derek James)

'No other military aircraft extant inspires so much awed admiration as does Avro's graceful Vulcan long-range medium bomber. This mighty aircraft has now graced five successive SBAC Flying Displays, yet familiarity never reduces the astonishing incredulity that greets its appearance. Having recently entered service with RAF Bomber Command, this powerful and, by bomber standards, unorthodox warplane recognises no better. It may be stated without fear of contradiction that the Vulcan B1 is the most potent medium bomber yet to attain service status anywhere in the world.'

Wg Cdr 'Roly' Falk, speaking in 1959

Early Vulcans that were delivered to the RAF were repainted overall anti-radiation white, except for the lower part of the nose radome, as XA900 shown here.

redesigned and greatly enlarged rear fuselage.

By 1957, it was clear that Vulcan, along with the other V-bombers, needed constant updating to perform its main task effectively. Radio countermeasure equipment (RCM) was introduced during production and modification, including Green Palm jammers to interfere with voice control of enemy fighter pilots, passive warning apparatus and tail

➤
A trio of early Vulcan B1s is seen prior to delivery. The kinked Phase 2 wing did not add to the Vulcan's performance, but allowed it to operate at high altitude and at high speed with a greater margin of safety.
(via Michael J.F. Bowyer)

warning Red Steer radar. Blue Diver ground radar jammer and Red Shrimp S-band noise jammer were installed. Radar warning equipment, including passive Blue Saga and rearward-looking Red Steer, was fitted in an enlarged tail cone. A flat, unpainted metal panel externally sited between the starboard engine pipes (extended to the port pipes later) was connected with Red Shrimp. 'Window' dispensers were also carried.

Vulcan B1 XH499 was operated by 230 Operational Conversion Unit. The RAF Waddington badge on its tail indicates its base.

The three V-bombers –
Victor, Vulcan and
Valiant – flying over
Farnborough in 1958.

On 5 May 1955, the Allied occupation of Germany having officially ended in the previous October, West Germany became a NATO member, just nine days before the USSR formed the Warsaw Pact between itself and Albania, Bulgaria, Czechoslovakia, East Germany, Hungary, Poland and Romania. 'Peaceful co-existence' was called for, but in reality the road to confrontation between East and West was well and truly laid.

Britain developed its own independent nuclear weapons programme, but on a much more modest scale than the USA and USSR. The strategy at the time, in the event of a Soviet strike, was for Allied ground forces to 'hold on' for three days at the most, prior to the USAF's Strategic Air Command (SAC) and RAF Bomber Command commencing a nuclear attack against selected cities in the USSR.

In 1955, as East–West tension heightened, the RAF bolstered its strategic nuclear bomber fleet available to NATO with the service debut of the Vickers Valiant. This was the first of the triumvirate of V-bombers to

▼ A B1A showing the new wing form with extended square-tipped wings.

reach Bomber Command's squadrons, being followed by the Handley Page Victor and Avro Vulcan, which were both operated in the strategic bomber and long-range reconnaissance roles. SAC received its first B-52 Stratofortress in June 1955, providing NATO with a still greater potential to respond to Soviet aggression.

The RAF's 'V-force' was built up through 1956–7, as first the Avro Vulcan, and then the Victor, began to reach Bomber Command squadrons in greater numbers. NATO's 'trip-wire' policy of launching an instant response using bombers and missiles in the event of a Soviet attack on any member country, meant that the integration of RAF Bomber Command's and SAC's strategic attack was all the more credible as a deterrent.

Bristol's success with the Olympus had, by the second half of the 1950s, forced a major redesign of the Vulcan's wing. The Mk 200 engine gave 16,000lb (71.2kN) thrust; this not only needed larger inlet ducts, but also a Phase 4 wing, with span increased by 12ft (3.66m) and a considerable reduction in thickness-chord ratio. These production Vulcan B2s also had provision for launching the Blue Steel rocket-propelled stand-off missile. The first seven B2s served as trials aircraft and were fitted with Olympus Mk 200 engines. By 1960, the 17,000lb st (75.6kN) Olympus Mk 201 was being installed, and the need for a rapid start-up and take-off led to a pneumatic engine-start system which, when fitted in 1961, changed the engine to Olympus Mk 202. Subsequently, production aircraft were fitted with the Olympus Mk 301 of 20,000lb (88.9kN)

◄
Trial installation of the Blue Steel rocket-propelled stand-off missile on Vulcan B1 XA903.
(via R.L. Ward)

Did you know?
The Vulcan is about the same size as a Boeing 737-200 airliner, although its delta wing makes it look much bigger. It weighs 95 tons fully laden, including 40 tons of fuel.

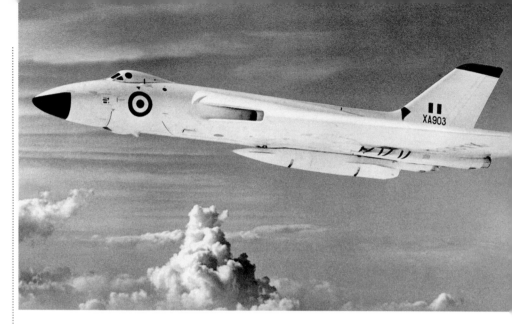

thrust. This gave a sprightly performance, but at low level, full power could not be used, except on take-off. Most Mk 301- powered aircraft served at Waddington, whereas the Scampton-based wing had Mk 201s.

◀
. . . while on the B2 the Blue Steel was partly recessed.

'The Vulcan was the most marvellous aeroplane. It really didn't have any vices. You had to work at getting it into trouble. The Vulcan could do just about anything — loop and barrel roll with a gay abandon that belied its size, turn on a sixpence at 50,000ft or 500ft, or beat up an airfield at over 400kts. The Vulcan looked right and flew right.'

Andrew Brookes, Vulcan pilot

35

The introduction of new surface-to-air missile (SAM) systems presented a significant threat to any aircraft penetrating Soviet airspace, and the availability to the USSR of ICBMs capable of hitting targets in the USA was heightening the West's anxiety. In terms of more conventional weapons, MiG-21 Fishbeds started to enter service with Russia's Frontal Aviation in 1959, while the Russian Long-Range Aviation received Tupolev Tu-95 Bear bombers, providing an extended strategic capability.

Tension mounted on 1 May 1960, when the Soviet SAMs shot down a Lockheed U-2C, being flown by CIA pilot Francis Gary Powers over Sverdlovsk, Russia. This halted the programme of US overflights by U-2s that had been taking place for a number of years. Six days after the shootdown the Soviet government announced that it had established a new Rocket Force Command.

The most serious 'flashpoint' occurred during 1962. Following the Bay of Pigs débâcle, when a US-sponsored invasion of Cuba by exiles had failed, the supply of arms by the Soviet Union to Fidel Castro's regime began in earnest. U-2 flights confirmed the presence of intermediate-range ballistic missiles and Tu-16 Badger bombers, which could easily reach the US mainland. Eventually the Soviets withdrew the weapons and conflict was averted at the eleventh hour.

It was announced in May 1963 that Supreme Allied Commander Europe (SACEUR) was to have under his command all of the RAF's operational V-bombers. In the same year the signing of the Moscow Treaty by the UK, USA and USSR banned nuclear tests in the atmosphere, outer space and under water. The involvement of the Soviet Union in the talks marked the start of the period of relative détente between the superpowers.

◄◄
On the other side, Russian Long-Range Aviation started to receive Tupolev Tu-95 Bear bombers in the early 1960s.

The completion of the twenty-ninth and final Vulcan B1 in October 1959 was immediately followed by the introduction of the B2, with much-modified airframe and uprated engines. A total of thirty-nine B2s had been ordered by 22 January 1958.

The first Vulcan B2 to be delivered to the RAF was XH558, joining No. 230 OCU on 1 July 1960, while the first front-line delivery was to No. 83 Squadron in December 1960. The Air Council, on 7 December 1961, approved a scheme whereby each V-force bomber squadron had to maintain one (subsequently increased to two) Vulcans at fifteen minutes' QRA (Quick Reaction Alert) readiness, its crew dressed in flying suits at cockpit readiness, and occupying a caravan close to their bombed-up aircraft.

Readiness was regularly tested by exercises such as 'Mayflight' and 'Micky Finn', these involving force-wide scrambles, dispersals and sustained operations. As a result 1962–3 saw the V-force at its strongest and highest state of readiness. By 1965, the V-force strength had fallen to eighty-eight aircraft, with about seventy Vulcans. The B1As were phased out by 1967.

Of the eighty-eight B2s that were flown, half were fitted with the 17,000lb st (76.2kN) Olympus 201 and the remainder with 20,000lb st (89.6kN) Olympus 301s. A total of twenty-six built with the capability of carrying the Blue Steel stand-off weapon were designated B2A, but returned to the standard configuration in 1969–70.

The final B2 (XM657) was completed at the end of 1964 and delivered to the RAF in the following January. This brought total Vulcan production to 136, which included the static fatigue-test airframe.

◄◄
A line-up of Vulcan B2s on the ORP (Operational Readiness Platform) at RAF Finningley.

Did you know?

Vulcans regularly provided targets for NATO's interceptor forces, and at extreme altitude could usually outmanoeuvre their pursuers (including the RAF's Lightnings). Heights of 65,000ft could sometimes be achieved under optimum conditions.

◄

RAF Vulcan B2s maintained the Quick Reaction Alert deterrent role until replaced by the Royal Navy's Polaris IRBM fleet.

(via Michael J.F. Bowyer)

End of the road for many of the Vulcan B1As was RAF St Athan, where they were scrapped in 1967.

Following their entry into operational service in 1957, the RAF's Vulcans constituted the sharp end of Britain's nuclear deterrent. This lasted until 1969, when the responsibility was handed over to the Royal Navy with its Polaris ICBM-capable submarines.

The first weapon for the V-force was the Blue Danube free-fall atomic bomb of about 20 kilotons explosive equivalent. However,

A Blue Steel on its cradle ready to be lifted under a Vulcan B2.
(Jeremy Flack/API)

on 16 June 1954 the British government initiated development of a more powerful interim 1-megaton atomic bomb, codenamed 'Violet Club' – effectively a Blue Danube casing fitted with the new Green Grass fission warhead. This was a stop-gap weapon (only twelve were made), which was assembled from March 1958 by technicians from the Atomic Weapons Research Establishment (AWRE) at Aldermaston (and not from the RAF), as Violet Club was subject to serious handling restrictions and remained under the custody and control of AWRE.

In order to accommodate the new Blue Steel stand-off weapon, the Scampton wing's Vulcans were modified to B2A standard, with provision for the semi-recessed Blue Steel and special bomb-bay doors. No. 617 Squadron received its first B2As in September 1961, and the Scampton wing eventually had a fleet

Vulcan B2 XL445 of No. 27 Squadron carrying Blue Steel.

of twenty-six Blue Steel-configured Vulcans. Following the cancellation of Skybolt, Cottesmore's aircraft were optimised for carriage of the WE177B lay-down strategic nuclear bomb. The WE177 came into service in 1966, while the Yellow Sun hydrogen bomb remained in service alongside it until 1972.

With a speed of Mach 2.3 and a range of 115 miles (185km), Blue Steel was intended to provide the V-bombers with a high-altitude weapon that did not lead them to expose themselves to the air defences of high-priority enemy targets. Blue Steel operational capability was achieved by No. 617 Squadron on 24 September 1962, following launch trials during the summer at the Woomera (Australia) ranges. By the end of 1964, Nos 27 and 83 Squadrons were similarly equipped, sharing weapons with the Wittering wing's Victor B2s.

The number of RAF Bomber Command squadrons operating Valiants, Victors and Vulcans reached a peak of twenty-two in 1963. However, the entire Valiant force was retired two years later with major metal fatigue concerns. After the US cancellation of Skybolt there was some uncertainty regarding the RAF's contribution to NATO's strategic deterrent. Some sixty Douglas Thor intermediate-range ballistic missiles, provided by the USA in 1958, were also being retired owing to the difficulty of operating them.

Although Blue Steel had in effect been rendered obsolete as a high-altitude weapon by Soviet surface-to-air missile (SAM) advances even before it entered service, it was adapted for low-level operations from mid-1964. Free-fall bombs were the only credible high-altitude nuclear weapons option for the Vulcan fleet.

◀
XH537 was used for a series of dummy Skybolt drops at the West Freugh range in 1969. A new Phase 6 wing would have carried six Skybolts on the proposed Vulcan B3.

➤

Blue Steel operational capability was achieved by No. 617 Squadron on 24 September 1962, following successful launch trials at the Woomera ranges in Australia during the summer.
(Rolls-Royce)

As the Vulcan's high-altitude role diminished, the RAF decided to modify its mission to meet current needs. From the mid-1960s until their retirement, Vulcans excelled in several new duties, most notably low-level nuclear strike and maritime reconnaissance.

The termination of the Skybolt programme, together with the proliferation of Soviet SAMs, combined to render existing high-altitude operations ineffective, at least beyond 1965. This created the UK's own 'missile gap' until such time as the Polaris force could become operational, which was expected to be in 1969. RAF Bomber Command was without any alternative other than to make the transition to low-level operations to maintain the V-force's survivability. This caused serious problems until the WE177B strategic parachute-retarded lay-down bomb could be brought into service. The Yellow Sun and Red Beard weapons required a pop-up to at least 12,000ft for release. Blue Steel launched at low level was limited in range. At first, the Yellow Sun force went low-level against primary targets in war scenarios, leaving Blue Steel to attack fringe sites.

The transition to low-level operations occurred almost simultaneously with the full entry into service of the Blue Steel missile. Avionics and self-defence systems were also revamped for low level. When Blue Steel was being carried, its inertial navigation system was so accurate that it became the prime navigation sensor, although a radar cross-check and other data updated its position information just before release.

In the conventional bombing role, the Vulcan carried up to three clips of seven bombs each. The bombs were sequenced to

Did you know?
After Skybolt was cancelled, the UK opted for Polaris. If Skybolt had been adopted, the proposed six-missile Vulcan B3 would have been developed to enable the RAF to undertake an alert deterrent with eighty-four Skybolts in the air at any one time.

In the conventional bombing role, the Vulcan carried up to three clips of seven bombs each. The 'iron' bombs were sequenced to drop singly from the clips, as shown here.
(via Michael J.F. Bowyer)

drop singly from each clip in the order front, centre and rear, repeating the sequence seven times.

On 30 June 1969, the Royal Navy's Polaris submarines took over the mantle of nuclear deterrent from the V-force, and the Scampton wing gave up its Blue Steel QRA role on 21 December 1970, when No. 617 Squadron flew the final Blue Steel sortie.

Rapid getaway and standing patrols in time of high tension continued, but the Vulcans now flew as low as possible to evade defences and detection, before the necessary 'pop-up' to release weapons from 2,500ft to 8,500ft. Terrain-following radar was fitted, along with the latest navigation aids, such as the Decca roller map and Green Satin, which gave continuous information on track, ground speed and distance flown. Protection came from ECM – passive, active and assorted jammers. Infrared decoy flares could be released, as well as rapid-blooming Window.

A tactical nuclear and increased conventional role was then assumed by the Vulcans, while the Victor aircraft were converted for strategic reconnaissance and air-to-air refuelling duties. The Canberra B(I)8s based in Germany then provided the RAF's only tactical bombing element assigned to NATO.

Following the Vulcan's switch to low-level operations, the overall anti-flash white livery was replaced by matt grey/green camouflage on the upper surfaces.

➤
Concorde's Olympus 593 engine was carried underneath Vulcan B1 XA903 and it was first flown in this guise from Filton on 9 September 1966.

Did you know?

While Vulcan B1 XA903 was flight-testing the RB199 engine for the Tornado, a Mauser cannon was fitted to the starboard nacelle to test the effect of firing on the engine's performance. Thereby XA903 became the only Vulcan ever to fire a gun.

The Vulcan's large size, together with excellent ground clearance, high speed and outstanding altitude capability made it a natural testbed aircraft for high-performance jet engines. Specially instrumented, Vulcan B1 XA903 played a major part in the development of engines for three of the UK's most important aircraft programmes – the Olympus 22R for the supersonic BAC TSR.2 (which was disastrously cancelled in the mid-1960s), the Olympus 593 for Concorde and finally the Rolls-Royce/Turbo-Union RB199 for the Panavia Tornado. Additionally, XA894 was to have tested the BS100 vectored-thrust engine for the Hawker P.1154, but the trials were cancelled following the axing of the entire supersonic VTOL programme. XA903 logged over

▼
Vulcan B1 XA894 testbed, fitted with an afterburning Olympus 22R for the BAC TSR2 under its fuselage. The engine had a bifurcated intake to cater for the Vulcan's nosewheel. The aircraft was destroyed at Filton when test engines exploded during ground running in December 1962.

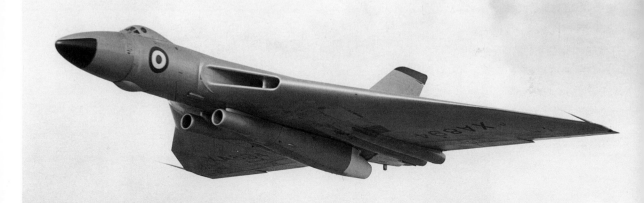

400 hours of test flying with an Olympus 593, in a Concorde engine-pod beneath the fuselage, before the supersonic airliner flew in 1969. One Vulcan B2, XH557, was used by Bristol Siddeley for routine engine-development flying in the early 1960s. On 27 February 1979, testbed XA903 made the last flight of a Vulcan B1.

➤
XA903 later carried the Panavia Tornado's Rolls-Royce RB199 engine.

◄
Close-up of the RB199 on full reheat. On 27 February 1979, XA903's final flight was the last made by a Vulcan B1.

57

The Non-Proliferation Treaty on Nuclear Weapons came into effect on 5 March 1970, and in the same year negotiations opened in Vienna on the Strategic Arms Limitation Treaty (SALT), of which one of the most important aspects was the limit on defensive anti-missile forces. The signing of the SALT agreement by US president Richard Nixon and the Soviet leader, Leonid Brezhnev, took place in Moscow in May 1972. This set new limits on ballistic missile deployments and offensive capability, but the mood of optimism that ensued was premature. The West's concern in the late 1970s centred on the continuing expansion of the Warsaw Pact's armed forces, and their apparent improved capabilities. On 11 March 1985, Mikhail Gorbachev became Communist Party leader. A much younger man, he was known to have some inclination towards modernisation of the USSR as its economy began to slow down. Gorbachev was to preside over the most dramatic shift in Soviet policy and oversaw the events of 1989 that were to change the face of Europe. In 1985 Gorbachev began to speak of *Perestroika*, a major programme of economic redevelopment, and *Glasnost*, a new Soviet political openness in both internal and external affairs. In October 1986, at a summit with President Reagan at Reykjavik in Iceland, new agreements were made, and in December 1987 at the Washington summit, it was announced that all long-range and short-range intermediate nuclear weapons were to be destroyed.

On 9 November 1989, the Berlin Wall, the most significant symbol of the Iron Curtain, was torn down. Germany was reunified in October 1990. The Soviet economy became still weaker, leading to the collapse of the USSR in 1991, and the Cold War finally came to an end.

Vulcan B2 XJ783 was based at RAF Akrotiri, Cyprus, with the Near East Air Force.

Reconnaissance had been a role assigned to the V-force since its inception, with Valiants and Victors performing the task with No. 543 Squadron. The mission had substantially changed from photo to radar reconnaissance, and the emphasis had shifted to maritime operations. With the release of surplus Vulcan airframes from the run-down of the airborne nuclear force, the type became available for long-range maritime radar reconnaissance sorties. The Vulcan B2's bomb/navigation radar (which had received a much greater sidescan capability with the introduction of the low-level role) was the primary sensor, backed up by cameras. The Vulcan's long range, together with its excellent low-level handling, made it ideal for the task. No. 27 Squadron was re-formed on 1 November 1973 as the dedicated MRR squadron with nine modified Vulcan

No. 27 Squadron Vulcan B2(MRR) on patrol from RAF Scampton over the North Sea oil rig Trans World 58 in August 1976. (via R.L. Ward)

B2(MRR)s. The other two units of the Scampton wing (Nos 35 and 617 Squadrons) also had MRR as a secondary tasking.

The discovery and subsequent exploitation of North Sea oil made the area one of strategic importance to the UK, warranting special attention from the Vulcan MRR fleet. The MRR version had Loran C navigation equipment added and the terrain-following radar 'pimple' removed from its nose. They also retained the gloss polyurethane camouflage paint when their bombing counterparts converted to a matt finish. Some had the underwing pylons activated for the occasional carriage of upper-air sampling pods. These were classified sensor systems (electronic, optical and others unspecified). The sampling portion of the pod was located at the front, consisting of an aperture that could be opened to begin sampling, behind which was a filter.

A small number of specially modified Vulcan B2s were operated in the Strategic Maritime Reconnaissance (MRR) role from November 1972 to May 1982.

By 1975, the RAF was looking towards the Panavia Tornado multi-role aircraft, still some six years away. During that time, Vulcans remained as an operational low-level force increasingly reliant upon non-nuclear retarded-fall HE bombs. Vulcan phase-out was planned for the first quarter of 1982. With the closure of No. 230 OCU at Scampton on 31 August 1981, the Vulcan's demise seemed near. On 31 December 1981, No. 617 Squadron disbanded as a Vulcan squadron, followed on 26 February 1982 by No. 35, and on 31 March 1982 by No. 27, which for ten years had undertaken maritime reconnaissance missions. Waddington's three squadrons were scheduled to close at the end of June 1982. Suddenly, an unexpected event shattered the plan when, on 2 April 1982, Argentina invaded the Falkland Islands. Disbandment plans were halted, and eleven days later four Vulcan crews began air-to-air refuelling training with Marham's Victor tankers and practised dropping 1,000lb bombs. Within the final days of its active service career the Vulcan was, astonishingly, going to drop bombs in anger.

Twenty-five years after it first entered service, the Vulcan went into action in 1982 during Operation 'Corporate', the UK campaign to recover the Falkland Islands. Faced with the enormous distances involved between the available bases, the RAF's Vulcans, with the aid of Victor tankers, were the only RAF aircraft that could be used in the attack role from the nearest land base, Wideawake airfield on Ascension Island. From here the first Operation 'Black Buck' bombing raids were launched against the islands on 30 April/1 May and 3/4 May. It took at least twelve Victor K2 tanker sorties to get the Vulcans on target and safely back to Ascension.

The priority was to deny the Argentine force the use of Port Stanley airfield for high-performance tactical aircraft, so the first two Black Buck raids were aimed at damaging the runway. After a high-altitude transit from Ascension, Vulcan XM607 (operating at an overload weight of 210,000lb/95,256kg) descended to low level for the approach to the islands before popping up to cross the target. A stick of twenty-one bombs was then released at an angle to the direction of the runway, in the hope of landing at least

◀

Vulcan B2 XM607, which flew the first Black Buck mission from Ascension Island to the Falklands and back, dropping twenty-one 1,000lb bombs on Port Stanley airfield.

> XM607's bomb bay, showing four of the twenty-one bombs it carried and the additional fuel tanks fitted for the Falklands raid in May 1982.

Did you know?

Avro's Vulcan was conceived for a deadly mission: nuclear bombing of the Soviet Union. When it finally went into action in the twilight of its career, it was in a very different scenario: attacking a runway 8,000 miles (12,874km) from its base.

one bomb directly on the surface. In this the first raid was successful. The mission had lasted 15 hours 45 minutes for the 7,500-mile (12,070km) round trip. An anti-runway attack by the second Black Buck mission was not successful, but the flights had shown that Port Stanley was not a safe place for Argentinian aircraft, and no fast jets were ever deployed there.

With that objective achieved, the Vulcans were then used in the anti-radar role (against TPS-43F, TPS-44 and Skyguard installations) in further raids – Black Buck 4, 5 and 6. The penultimate attack was flown on 2/3 June 1982, and destroyed a Skyguard radar, although the Vulcan (XM597) made a dramatic diversion into Rio de Janeiro after its refuelling probe broke. Black Buck 7, on 11/12 June, delivered airburst bombs.

'We were launched from Wideawake late on 2 June, this time armed with four Shrikes for another attack against the Falklands. We commenced the final run-in during the early hours of 3 June and some forty minutes were spent waiting overhead for the radar to be switched on. The aircraft's RWR picked up an Ejercito Skyguard radar and two Shrikes were launched, destroying the radar which had been acting as a fire control unit for one of the GADA 601 anti-aircraft batteries close to Port Stanley. Due to a critical fuel state we were forced to leave the area and assisted by a Nimrod MR2 we made a successful rendezvous with our Victor tanker about half-way back to Wideawake. However, the tip of the Vulcan's refuelling probe broke off during the AAR and we were forced to divert to the nearest airfield – Rio de Janeiro in Brazil.'

Sqn Ldr C.N. McDougall, pilot of XM597 engaged on a Black Buck raid.

Vulcan B2 XM597 that flew on the penultimate Black Buck mission against Argentinian anti-aircraft defences near Port Stanley.

XM597 made a dramatic diversion into Rio de Janeiro, Brazil, after its refuelling probe broke away while taking fuel from a Victor tanker during its return journey.

Close-up of the mission markings on the nose of XM597, representing the two Shrike missile attacks made against Argentinian radar installations.

The Black Buck missions were among the longest bombing missions in history (and the longest for the RAF) based on straight-line distances. Thus ended the Vulcans' finest hour. Little material damage had been caused by the raids, despite the immense tanker effort and expense to mount them. However, the 1 May attack had been a spectacular opening to the British recapture effort and a warning that – even though the Port Stanley runway was swiftly repaired – basing combat aircraft there would be unwise.

Before the end of 1982, two of the three surviving squadrons had disbanded. No. 101 Squadron closed down on 4 August, and No. 44 Squadron on 21 December.

Vulcan B2 XM575 of No. 44 Squadron, the last Vulcan bomber unit, which was disbanded on 21 December 1982.

*Vulcan B2 XM594 of
No. 44 Squadron.*
(Graham Finch)

Did you know?
The Vulcan holds the record for the longest bombing mission by any British military aircraft: 7,700 miles from Ascension Island to the Falklands and return. On one of these missions the Vulcan carried twenty-one 1,000lb conventional high-explosive bombs for attacks on Stanley airfield. Similar missions were also flown carrying Shrike anti-radiation missiles to take out the Argentinian air defence radar.

The Vulcan adopted a new role in the twilight of its career. Six Vulcans were returned to Woodford in 1982 for conversion to air-to-air refuelling tankers.
(BAe)

Like the Valiant and the Victor before it, the Vulcan adopted the role of tanker in the twilight of its career. In 1982, with the Falklands campaign in full swing, a large percentage of the Victor tanker force was needed at Ascension Island, leaving the UK base fleet sorely depleted. The only means of partially restoring the situation was the hasty conversion of six Vulcan bombers (of which XH558 was one), a task carried out at BAe Woodford.

XH561, the first of the six aircraft earmarked, arrived at Woodford on 4 May 1982, flying again on 18 June, four days after the Argentinian surrender. Delivered to No. 50 Squadron on 23 June, it undertook its first operational sortie on 30 June. The type served until March 1984, by which time sufficient VC10s had been converted to take over the tanker role.

◄
The tankers' HDU drogue basket, bolted on at the rear, deployed aerodynamically but was reeled in by an electro-hydraulic motor.

Did you know?

The last six Vulcans in service with the RAF were converted for the air-to-air refuelling role prior to the introduction of VC10 tankers.

Three fuel tanks filled the Vulcan B2's bomb bay, shown here in XH558, photographed at Greenham Common in July 1983.
(Brian Strickland)

XM571, another of the six K2 conversions flown by No. 50 Squadron, refuelling an RAF Buccaneer S2B.
(Flight Refuelling Ltd)

The conversion involved the removal of the ECM installation and the fitment of a large, entirely unaerodynamic box below the tail to house a Mk 17B flight refuelling hose-drum unit. The bomb bay was filled with three auxiliary tanks of 1,000 gal (4,546 litres) capacity each, complementing the aircraft's normal load of 9,200 gal (41,823 litres) in the wing tanks.

No. 50 Squadron operated only in the northern hemisphere during its short career as a tanker unit, disbanding on 31 March 1984. It had flown 3,000 hours in the tanker role, but was already depleted by the removal of hose-drum units to feed the VC10 tanker version on the conversion line at BAe Filton.

◄
XH558, the last Vulcan to fly with the RAF, was another tanker conversion flown by No. 50 Squadron until early 1984.

◄◄
The Vulcan Display Flight's B2 XL426 refuelling from XH560 during a training flight from Waddington.

XH558

The vast majority of Vulcans met their end at the hands of the scrapman's torch at RAF St Athan, or were relegated to trainer airframes with RAF battle-damage repair flights, or with RAF station fire sections and the Central Fire School at Catterick. The first round of scrapping came with the retirement of the B1A fleet, which assembled at St Athan in 1966 for disposal and sale as scrap. A similar fate greeted many B2s in 1981/2 as the Vulcan force wound down. With a relatively low scrap price, down to about £5,000, a number of airframes were acquired by museums and collections, and the RAF preserved a selection for donations to museums. Unfortunately, no complete examples of the Vulcan B1/B1A have survived. A number of nose sections have been saved.

◄

Like the Vulcan B1As, most of the retired B2s were flown to RAF St Athan and were sold for scrap for as little as £5,000 each.
(Jeremy Flack/API)

For more than a quarter of a century, air show crowds were used to seeing an RAF Vulcan as a star attraction. Towards the end of the V-bomber's service life a designated aircraft was operated by the Vulcan Display Team (VDT). When the big delta was finally retired by the RAF in 1984, the Ministry of Defence decided to keep one aircraft, at that time XL426, airworthy for air display purposes with the Vulcan Display Team at RAF Waddington.

However, Vulcan XL426's flying hours were rapidly running out and a major over-haul was looming, so XH560 was designated as its replacement. But this aircraft was found to have only 160 hours left, whereas Vulcan tanker XH558, which had been flown to RAF Marham on 17 September 1984, earmarked for scrapping, had nearly four times the flying hours remaining.

◄
XL426 was the first aircraft to be earmarked by the RAF for the display team. This aircraft is now at Southend and makes regular ground runs.
(Andrew P. March)

Replacement aircraft for the Vulcan Display Team was XH558, which had more airframe hours remaining, despite having been the first B2 to be delivered to the RAF, and served to the end as a tanker.

▶▶
In 1987 the Vulcan Display Flight was established at Waddington to operate XH558 at air shows from 1988.

Did you know?

The Vulcan remains the only mass-produced large tailless delta aircraft in the world. The shape of the Vulcan is very close to the blended-wing body configuration that is now being investigated for the next generation of quiet, clean and efficient commercial airliners.

On 14 November 1984 XH558 was chosen as the future display aircraft and returned to Waddington for service engineered modification (SEM) conversion back to B2 configuration. This took place through the winter of 1984/5. XH558 then became as it would have been in its operational role as a bomber in the V-force.

Its first flight after conversion took place in April 1985, and in September, the Vulcan was flown to RAF Kinloss for repainting. It emerged resplendent in a high-gloss camouflage scheme, with the City of Lincoln coat of arms on its tail, along with the Union Jack. It also carried the black panther's head emblem of No. 1 Group, RAF Strike Command on both sides of the fuselage ahead of the engine intakes. XH558 returned to Waddington on 30 November 1985 and replaced XL426 as the display aircraft in May 1986,

making its first appearance at the TVS Air Show at Bournemouth (Hurn).

During the winter of 1987 it became increasingly difficult to keep the Vulcan airworthy on a volunteer basis and a request was made to establish the VDT formally. Prior to the start of the 1988 display season, approval was given for the establishment of the Vulcan Display Flight (VDF), to include seven engineering tradesmen to maintain the aircraft for the remainder of its service life.

By the end of the 1991 air show season, XH558 had the highest flying time of any Vulcan airframe, at almost 7,300 hours. Its fatigue life was down to less than 10 FI (fatigue index) with an annual usage of approximately 7 FI, which meant it was close to being grounded. A review of the fatigue index figures carried out in conjunction with British Aerospace (BAe), as successor company to Avro, the Vulcan's design authority, resulted in an increased allowance of fatigue index. This was sufficient to permit a safe margin to undertake displays through the 1992 season. With a major service due at 7,401 flying hours, and the aircraft being almost life-expired on fatigue index, flying beyond the end of 1992 looked doubtful.

The Ministry of Defence revealed that two engineering tasks would need to be undertaken to enable XH558 to continue flying: plate-strengthening modifications to the front and rear spars, which would increase the FI to a figure sufficient for another eight to ten years, and a major service, which would give the airframe more than enough flying hours to allow that FI to be consumed. At the same time, the MOD said that it had been decided that work on the main spar, or its replacement, was not required.

Unfortunately, the sting was in the last part of the announcement: 'At the present time it appears most unlikely that the RAF will have the necessary funds available to complete this essential work.' The full overhaul that would have permitted the Vulcan a further 1,280 training/flying hours would have been very costly. XH558's last major overhaul by the RAF had taken about 24,000 man-hours to complete in the early

<<

As a tribute to the Vulcan, the Red Arrows escorted XH558 to its final display.
(BAe)

 On 20 September 1992, during its final public performance, XH558 displayed in formation with the Red Arrows aerobatic team.

▶▶
The final flypast on 20 September revealed the word 'FAREWELL' (as distinct from 'Goodbye') to the assembled crowd as it opened its bomb doors in flight for the last time.

1980s. This had been on the line at St Athan with all the necessary equipment, special tools, replacement parts and 'consumables' readily available. Completing this task on its own without the engineering infrastructure would inevitably be more costly and was estimated at about £2.5 million.

When the MOD announced that it was not intending to fund more than routine winter servicing on XH558 after the 1992

season and the chances of obtaining financial support from elsewhere were thought
unlikely, it became clear that the Vulcan's
scheduled display at Cranfield on 20 September was likely to be its last.

Cranfield was packed for the Dream-
flight Air Show organised by Biggin Hill-
based Air Displays International. There was
little doubt that the star attraction was
Vulcan XH558 on its well-publicised final
public display outing. As a fitting introduction to its final performance, the big
delta made two passes flanked by the Red
Arrows. After that, it was put through its
paces in the familiar manner, concluding
with a final flypast, revealing the word
'FAREWELL' to the crowd as it opened its
bomb-bay doors.

After the end of the 1992 season, the MOD gave notice that the Vulcan would be sold by tender. This prompted an outcry from enthusiasts and members of the public calling for a real effort to be made to keep the world's last big delta flying. It is estimated that over 180,000 signatures were put to petitions and many individual letters sent to MPs from all parts of the UK. In response to this the MOD said that it would consider sustainable commercial proposals to keep the aircraft flying, both before and during the tendering process. In the meantime the Vulcan continued to make occasional flights from RAF Waddington in order to keep the crew current. The MOD said it was specifically to allow the Vulcan to be delivered by air to a new owner if it was sold, or to a designated airfield if it was to be overhauled.

There was much speculation about the possible options available for future operation of the Vulcan, but the well-intentioned proposals generally failed to address the underlying issues that had to be considered together as a complete package if XH558 was to be kept flying.

The MOD made it clear that XH558 could not be displayed in 1993, although it had approximately twenty flying hours available, because it had not undergone normal winter minor overhaul/servicing and that there were no funds allocated to the Vulcan in the 1993 defence budget for maintenance or display flying. In fact the MOD was expecting to receive funds from the Vulcan's sale.

Another obstacle emanated from the UK Civil Aviation Authority (CAA), when it indicated that it would not issue a permit for the Vulcan to be flown and displayed as

XH558 photographed by the press for the last time over Lincolnshire, marking the end of an era.

a civil-registered aircraft. This threw the Vulcan's future back to the MOD, who said that further operation of the Vulcan by the RAF could be done only in partnership with civilian organisations, who would have to provide a viable assurance that the financial, operating and technical requirements for the Vulcan could be met over the proposed additional 'lifetime'.

Since the design authority for the Vulcan rested with British Aerospace, the company would have to be closely involved at every stage in servicing and maintaining the aircraft if it was to be operated by the RAF. Predictably the company had reservations about any open-ended commitment to do this.

As the Vulcan was constructed from materials of 1950 to 1960s specification, there was some uncertainty about the condition deep within the aircraft's structure. Neither the RAF nor BAe could guarantee that major corrosion or other problems might not be unearthed once the Vulcan was fully stripped down. Four significant modifications to extend the Vulcan's 'fatigue life' also had to be undertaken during the essential overhaul. It was estimated that this task would take up to 3,400 man-hours.

Despite facing 'the north wall of the Eiger', as the daunting task of drawing up a viable commercial and operational plan to keep the Vulcan flying appeared to be, efforts were still being made to achieve this at the turn of the year. It all came to an abrupt end when Jonathan Aitken, Minister of State for Defence Procurement, said on 28 January 1993 that there was no further justification for delaying the sale of the aircraft. He said: 'Ministry officials have

met and corresponded with representatives of the public campaign to keep the Vulcan flying on a number of occasions since the middle of November to explain in detail the implications of the aircraft's continued operation. No new sponsorship proposals have been received during that period. It is expected that the sale of the Vulcan will be completed in about three months.'

An RAF spokesman said: 'Although we recognise the great deal of public affection for the Vulcan it would be uneconomic to give the aircraft major maintenance work for what would be one season's operation. Those who flew and maintained the Vulcans during their years of RAF service will remember them with great affection, as will the thousands who have attended airshows in recent years to see the last of the line.'

On 3 March 1993 a petition was handed in to Parliament by members of the 'Save the Vulcan' Campaign (see p. 95). It was presented by Gp Capt Harry Bromley, a former Vulcan pilot, to Harry Greenway, MP. A large-scale model of the Vulcan, built by Phil Cadwallader at Oldham, was transported from Lancashire to London as part of the campaign. Parading the model through the streets near to Parliament caused a certain amount of disruption and created substantial media interest. A few days later the MOD announced that Vulcan XH558 had been sold to the highest bidder.

'Save XH558' campaign supporters, led by Gp Capt Harry Bromley, carry a large-scale model of the Vulcan and a petition towards Parliament on 3 March 1993. This last-ditch attempt was unsuccessful.
(John Carpenter)

Vulcan B2 XH558 made its last flight with an RAF crew on 23 March 1993. This was a delivery flight to C. Walton Ltd at Bruntingthorpe, Leicestershire, who had purchased it from the MOD, along with a large stock of spares and equipment. David Walton, managing director of the firm and a keen Vulcan enthusiast, had bought the former V-bomber with the aim of returning it to the air-show circuit under a CAA Permit to Fly.

After it arrived at the company-owned airfield, nothing was removed from the Vulcan, as the crew simply shut everything down, closed the door and handed over the key to its new owner. Over the next few months, some 650 tonnes of spares were purchased at obsolete-component cost from the RAF, together with the all-important documentation. The package also included the last eight unused Rolls-Royce Olympus 202 engines that had been stored at No. 16 MU, RAF Stafford.

Immediately after its arrival in March 1993, XH558 was hangared at Bruntingthorpe. From the outset, its systems were carefully maintained in operating condition by volunteers, including type-experienced engineers, working under licensed supervision. The Vulcan was brought out for occasional runs down the Bruntingthorpe runway on open days until 1999. At that time their aim was straightforward – give XH558 its 'major' service, some remedial work and review by the CAA, and return it to flight once again.

Dr Robert Pleming, an experienced technical manager and Vulcan enthusiast, had offered to help David Walton to explore the feasibility of returning XH558 to flight. Discussions with the Civil Aviation Authority (CAA) and British Aerospace (Avro, the original manufacturers of the aircraft, was now part of BAE Systems) led to the creation of a formal project, supported by the necessary documentation and procedures. This was to enable Robert Pleming's team to prove that the technical, commercial and operational management of the task of getting XH558 back into the air and operating it safely as a civilian aircraft was realistic.

Because the Vulcan was considered by the CAA to be a 'complex' aircraft for the purposes of obtaining a Permit to Fly, a CAA-approved (under BCAR A8-20) engineering organisation was required to carry out the Vulcan restoration, operation and maint-enance activities. The XH558 'Plan-to-Flight Project Team' decided, with the support of BAe, to continue working with Marshall of Cambridge Aerospace Ltd.

Two years later the Vulcan Operating Company (VOC) project team had reached an important point. In May 1999 BAe's board agreed to support XH558's return to flight. The critical path forward had been mapped out. A project definition workshop had completed a feasibility study and a risk assessment, and produced a project definition. This concluded that there was no technical barrier to returning the Vulcan to flight, and the project would be able to move on to the next phase – a pre-service technical survey (PSTS). Its objective would be to understand more fully and document the technical condition of the aircraft so that its restoration to flying condition could be planned in detail.

The PSTS was undertaken from late 1999. A group of engineers from Marshalls at Cambridge, together with VOC engineers, stripped the Vulcan down to its bare framework, removing its engines, systems and components. While the survey did find some

◄◄
XH558 was stripped in the hangar at Bruntingthorpe and the task of making the airframe airworthy was carefully assessed.

problems, none were significant and known solutions to them were available. Some of the electronic systems associated with the former bomber's operational duties were found to be inoperative, but working replacement units were available. Most importantly, the aircraft's forty-year-old wiring was found to be in good condition. Some of the wiring terminations in exposed locations were found to be corroded but replaceable.

The aircraft's structure was seen to be suffering from the onset of corrosion in a few places; however, the levels were measured to be well below the point at which aircraft strength would be compromised. XH558's original equipment manufacturers (OEMs), who numbered over a hundred, were contacted, and they agreed to assess and service components as required.

Following from this technical survey, a detailed report on their findings was drawn by the design authority (BAE Systems Chadderton), the designated engineering organisation (Marshall of Cambridge Aerospace) and the VOC. This set out what maintenance action above and beyond the major service would be required, given the age of XH558 and the time since its last flight. From completion of the technical survey, it was established that with appropriate regulatory approvals and the technical support by BAE Systems, the aircraft could be returned to flying order. All that was required to make aviation history was the necessary funding.

By 2000, David Walton's family business had already funded the project to the tune of £500,000 but had now reached the end of the road. It was clear that it was going to cost a great deal more to get XH558 airborne again

◄

At the beginning of 2006, the huge task of reassembling XH558 was well under way.
(Kev Storer)

than the sums that were then forthcoming from voluntary donations. David Walton, Robert Pleming and colleagues set about finding ways to bring in more money to the project. Failure to do this, they warned, could result in the Vulcan being sold to an interested American purchaser. This brought a strong response from a lot of people and, in particular, Felicity Irwin, who was so resolved that such a valuable British heritage asset should not be allowed to leave the country that she joined the project team to run the fundraising and PR campaign.

➤
Dr Robert Pleming has led the project team through its various stages to achieve the return of the Vulcan to the sky.

Since that time, the Vulcan to the Sky (VTS) programme has been introduced and hundreds of thousands of pounds have been raised. With several million pounds needed, it was soon apparent that a major financial supporter had to be found. The VTS team believed it appropriate that the UK Heritage Lottery Fund (HLF) should be the funding body for such a valuable heritage asset, so an application was made in 2002. However, this bid was rejected towards the end of the year.

Following a vigorous and very critical response from the public to its decision, the HLF provided specific and detailed feedback on how the application could be enhanced to maximise the long-term public benefits. A revised application was submitted in May 2003. This included an education programme that would take the story of the Cold War, in which the Vulcan stands as an important symbol, to the widest possible audience. Despite having a policy not to support projects whose aim is the restoration of aircraft to flight, the HLF trustees announced in December 2003, to a delighted VTS team and their supporters, that they had made an 'exceptional decision' and a 'stage one pass' to earmark a grant of £2.5m for the programme was approved.

On 23 June 2004, the HLF announced that it had awarded £2.734m to the VTS project, thus enabling the administrative processes to get under way. The first of these was to purchase XH558 for the nation from its owner, C. Walton Ltd. The purchase, on 3 March 2005, allowed the Vulcan to the Sky Trust (VTST) to proceed with the preparations to get the Vulcan flying. The HLF grant, together with the partnership funding raised by donation, corporate support and fundraising will eventually help to make up the £3.97m required.

The VTST also entered into partnership with Marshall of Cambridge Aerospace Ltd to manage the project, and it teamed up with the Royal Air Force Charitable Trust Enterprises for merchandising, the Vulcan 558 Club for volunteer support, and the Imperial War Museum, Duxford.

Before work could begin on the Vulcan at Bruntingthorpe, there were some important preliminaries that had to be carried out in the first half of 2005. The hangar itself had to be prepared to meet the airworthiness regulations and quality processes that control the engineering environment in which the restoration took place. It had to be brought up to the same high standard as those used for the maintenance of civil airliners. The CAA checked that the cleanliness, lighting, health and safety, signage, tools and working procedures met its audit requirements before anyone started work.

The hangar and Vulcan were handed over to Marshalls in June 2005, and staff were recruited and trained. It formally became an outstation of the company's facilities at Cambridge Airport and was linked electronically with its support systems and controls when work finally started in August 2005.

There were four well-defined, but overlapping phases drawn up to take the Vulcan through to its first flight. This 'major service', which mirrored the most in-depth and extensive overhaul activity carried out by the RAF while the bomber was on its strength, was expanded to cover a number of additional areas of investigation, as a result of the length of time since its last 'major' at RAF St Athan in 1981. In addition, key components and systems that had been sent to their original manufacturers for servicing had to be serviced or replaced and returned. Engines were not a problem, since there were two 'new' zero-hours sets of four Olympus 202 turbojets available for installation.

The first 'Inspection' phase got under way in August 2005. Every part of the aircraft was subjected to a comprehensive and minute inspection according to well-defined procedures, to discover whether there were any problems. Included were a series of non-destructive testing (NDT) examinations of critical parts of the aircraft, such as the spars and the wing leading edge, using X-ray, ultrasound, eddy-current (which detects cracks in metal magnetically) and other advanced processes.

The inspection inevitably threw up a number of problems that needed rectification, including the repair or replacement of components, or the manufacture of new items. During this 'Rectification' phase, the second part of the 'major' was carried out. This involved the addition of a strengthening plate to the rear spar. Fortunately the VOC had a Vulcan spares holding of over 16,000 line items.

Once the rectification neared completion, the third, 'Recovery', phase started. This brought all the components and systems that were taken from the aircraft back to be reinstalled. The Vulcan's radios and avionics were upgraded, including the installation of a GPS (Global Positioning System), at this stage.

With the aircraft back together for the first time since 2000, the crucial 'Testing' phase was ready to begin. Following a pattern honed over many years of RAF service, a system-by-system test was completed on each part of the former V-bomber. Everything was thoroughly tested on the ground to ensure that it functioned correctly, and was in harmony with all the other systems. At the end of the ground test the aircraft could be released by the certifying engineers as being ready for flight test. All that was then needed was for the correct paperwork to be in place and the satisfactory completion of a final audit by the CAA before a Permit to Fly for test purposes could be issued. The CAA had to be convinced that the aircraft was satisfactory for flight under civilian regulations.

At the point that it was ready to fly, the project to get Vulcan XH558 back in the air had taken over 35,000 man-hours of aircraft engineer and fitter time, including rectification, and some 10,000 man-hours of design engineering time. This all cost a great deal of money. While many of the original manufacturers were committed to overhauling their Vulcan components free of charge, the technical and design teams working on XH558 were all made up of people holding scarce and valuable skills. The total cost was now over £3.1m.

Although the Vulcan was last airborne in 1993 and there were no 'current' aircrew, the VOC had on its team a number of the aircrew – pilots, air engineers, navigators – who flew the Vulcan during its service life with the RAF. It had long been decided that VOC's chief pilot, Sqn Ldr David Thomas, who made the last Vulcan flight on 23 March 1993, would be in the left-hand seat for the post-restoration flight, accompanied by CAA pilot Al McDicken, with Barry Masefield as AEO.

Returning Avro Vulcan B2 XH558 to the sky is an enormous task. It is the culmination of years of incredibly hard work by a small team of dedicated enthusiastic professionals. They wanted to preserve one of the icons of our twentieth-century aviation heritage so that it can be seen by many people all around the UK.

In addition to the personal sacrifices made to make the 'Vulcan to the Sky' dream become a reality, it has also required a great deal of money. To enable XH558 to fly for the next ten years or so, more funds will be needed.

To find out how you can support the Vulcan to the Sky Trust write to:

VTST, PO Box 3240, Wimborne, Dorset BH21 4YP, UK;

tel: 0800 083 2022; email: vulcantothesky@aol.com

or visit the website: www.vulcantothesky.com.

APPENDIX I – SPECIFICATION

VULCAN B1/B1A

Span:	99ft 0in (30.17m)
Length:	97ft 1in (29.59m)
Height:	26ft 6in (7.95m)
Wing area:	3,554sq ft (330.17m^2)
Service ceiling:	55,000ft
Range (without refuelling):	3,000 miles (4,825km)
Maximum speed:	625mph (1,006km/h – Mach 0.95 at 40,000ft
Cruising speed:	607mph (977km/h)
Maximum take-off weight:	190,000lb (86.18kg)
Crew:	5
Armament (carried internally):	Conventional – up to 21,000lb (9,526kg) of bombs
	Nuclear – one Blue Danube 10,000lb (4,536kg) atomic bomb initially, or later one 7,000lb (3,175kg) Yellow Sun Mk 1 or Mk 2 hydrogen bomb.

Engines:

First prototype:	Four 6,500lb st Rolls-Royce Avon R.A.3
	Four 8,000lb st Armstrong Siddeley Sapphire
	Four 15,000lb st Rolls-Royce Conway R.Co.7
Second prototype:	Four 9,750lb st Bristol Olympus 100
Vulcan B1:	Four 11,000lb st Bristol Olympus 101
	Four 12,000lb st Bristol Olympus 102
	Four 13,500lb st Bristol Olympus 104
XA902 only:	Four 17,250lb st Rolls-Royce Conway R.Co.11
XA891 only:	Four 16,000lb st Bristol Olympus 200

VULCAN B2

Span:	111ft 0in (33.83m)
Length:	100ft 1in (30.50m)
Height:	27ft 2in (8.29m)
Wing area:	3,964sq ft (368.3m^2)
Service ceiling:	65,000ft
Range (without refuelling):	4,600 miles (7,400km)
Maximum speed:	645mph (1,038km/h – Mach 0.95 at 40,000ft
Cruising speed:	625mph (1,006km/h – Mach 0.84)
Maximum take-off weight:	204,000lb (92,534kg)
Take-off-run:	3,500ft (1,067m) fully loaded
Time to 40,000ft:	9 min
Crew:	5
Armament (carried internally):	Conventional – up to 21,000lb (9,526kg) of bombs.
	Nuclear – one Avro Blue Steel Mk 1 stand-off missile or one 7,000lb (3,175kg) Yellow Sun Mk 2 free-fall hydrogen bomb or one WE177 A or B weapon. Many aircraft also included underwing attachment points for the Skybolt missile, which could later be used for the carriage of Shrike missiles and ECM pods.

Engines:	
XH533:	Four 6,500lb st Rolls-Royce Avon R.A.3
Vulcan B2:	Four 17,000lb st (75.66kN) Rolls-Royce (Bristol) B.O.16 Olympus 201
	Four 20,000lb st (88.96kN) Rolls-Royce (Bristol) B.O.121 Olympus 301

1947 7 January: The day before it was agreed to go ahead with the British atomic bomb, specification B.35/46 was formally issued. Avro, along with Armstrong Whitworth, English Electric and Handley Page, received an invitation to tender for the jet bomber.

1947 March: Avro Type 698 first sketched out as a pure delta flying wing.

1947 28 July: Avro was rated clear leader at the tender design conference and a decision was reached to order its aircraft.

1948 Two prototype Avro 698 delta-wing bombers were ordered and assigned serials VX770 and VX777. Two one-third-scale trials aircraft (VX784 and VX790) were also ordered.

1952 July: The first production Vulcan B1s were ordered – a month before the prototype's initial flight.

1952 30 August: The first Vulcan prototype VX770 flown by test pilot 'Roly' Falk.

1952 1 September: VX770 went to Boscombe Down for handling trials.

1952 September: The Vulcan appeared several times at the 1952 SBAC Farnborough Air Show.

1952 2 October: The name 'Vulcan' was chosen by the Air Council for the bomber.

1952 3 October: Britain successfully exploded its first atomic device, code-named 'Hurricane', at the Monte Bello islands off the north-west coast of Australia.

1953	July: VX770 resumed flying after the installation of Armstrong Siddeley Sapphire ASSa.6 engines.
1953	3 September: The second Vulcan prototype ,VX777, fitted with Olympus 100 engines, joined the programme.
1955	4 February: XA889, the first production Vulcan, made its first flight, powered by Olympus 101s.
1955	February: VX777 was grounded for fitting the Phase 2 wing and acted as the B2 prototype. The first five B1s flew with the original straight wing.
1955	September: 'Roly' Falk startled the aviation world by rolling the Vulcan at the 1955 Farnborough SBAC display, despite the relatively limited power then available.
1955	5 October: VX777 flew with the revised wing leading edge. The leading edge sweep-back was reduced from 52 to 42 degrees at half-span but increased further outboard. Engine nacelles were extended.
1956	31 May: Ministerial approval was given for the Vulcan B2 with the Phase 4 wing.
1957	January: 230 OCU at RAF Waddington received its first Vulcan B1s, XA895 and XA898. Crew training began on 21 February.
1957	21 May: No. 83 Squadron was the first Vulcan squadron formed at RAF Waddington and received the first aircraft on 11 July.
1957	31 August: VX777 first flew in Phase 2C wing configuration.

1957	Britain exploded its first hydrogen bomb.
1958	No. 617 Squadron (the 'Dam Busters') was re-formed at RAF Scampton to operate the Vulcan.
1958	19 August: First flight of XH533, the first of eighty-nine B2 airframes built by Avro. A total of forty-one B1s (of which five were used for development work) had been built.
1959	30 April: The last Vulcan B1 was delivered to the RAF.
1960	1 July: The first Vulcan B2 (XH558) was delivered to 230 OCU at RAF Waddington.
1960	No. 44 Squadron was established at RAF Waddington.
1960	23 December: No. 83 Squadron received its first Vulcan B2.
1961	April: The re-formation of No. 27 Squadron with Vulcan B2s, receiving its first B2 on 1 September.
1961	No. 50 Squadron was formed at RAF Waddington.
1961	230 OCU moved to RAF Finningley, to make room for No. 101 Squadron, which made the reverse journey.
1962	1 January: The Quick Reaction Alert (QRA) was established.
1962	23 February: XA894 first flew fitted with Olympus 22R engines, later replaced by the 22R-1 with reheat.
1962	The Coningsby wing became the first user of the WE177B lay-down strategic nuclear weapon.

1962 March: Formation of No. 9 Squadron, the new wing at RAF Coningsby, followed by No. 12 Squadron in July and finally No. 35 Squadron in December.

1962 24 September: No. 617 Squadron received Blue Steel training missiles, a rocket-propelled stand-off weapon, which was designed to be air-launched 100 miles from its target.

1962 November: The US government cancelled the Douglas AGM-87A Skybolt programme.

1963 The V-force was assigned to NATO and given a part in the alliance's nuclear strike plan, but with full powers of reversion to national control for nuclear tasks.

1964 RAF Cottesmore became the home of Nos 9, 12 and 35 Squadrons.

1964 April: The first Vulcan B1A (XH505) appeared in a coat of green and grey disruptive camouflage at RAF Waddington. This replaced the overall 'anti-flash' white with its pale-coloured serials and insignia.

1965 14 January: The last production Vulcan, XM657, was delivered to No. 35 Squadron at RAF Cottesmore.

1966 The first Vulcan B1As arrived at No. 19 MU at St Athan for recovery of useful equipment before scrapping.

1969 Nos 9 and 35 Squadrons serve at RAF Akrotiri, Cyprus.

1969 30 June: The RAF relinquished the QRA deterrent role to the Royal Navy Polaris IRBM fleet.

1969 31 August: No. 83 Squadron disbanded at RAF Scampton.

1970	21 December: No. 617 Squadron flew the final Blue Steel sortie.
1973	1 November: Establishment of No. 27 Squadron as the Maritime Radar Reconnaissance (MRR) Unit. Its nine Vulcans were designated Vulcan B2MRR and remained in service for ten years.
1981	January: It was decided to disband all the remaining Vulcan squadrons between June 1981 and June 1982 as the Tornado began to enter widespread service.
1981	August: No. 230 OCU closed, followed by No. 617 Squadron in December, and No. 35 in February 1982.
1982	31 March: No. 27 Squadron flew the last Scampton Vulcan sortie and handed its maritime duties over to the Nimrod fleet.
1982	30 April/1 May: XM607 made the first Black Buck sortie to the Falkland Islands to make an attack on Port Stanley airfield.
1982	31 December: The last B2 squadron, No. 44, was disbanded.
1984	31 March: Vulcan K2s withdrawn from service.
1992	20 September: XH558 gave the last air display by an RAF Vulcan, at Cranfield.
1993	23 March: XH558 landed at Bruntingthorpe Airfield, Leicestershire, and was delivered to its new owner, C. Walton Ltd. Its delivery flight included flypasts over Woodford and former Vulcan bases. It was the last Avro Vulcan to leave RAF service.

PRESERVED IN THE UK

XH558/G-VLCN	B2	Vulcan to the Sky Trust, Bruntingthorpe
XJ823	B2	Solway Aviation Society, Edward Haughey Aviation Heritage Centre, Carlisle, Cumbria
XJ824	B2	Imperial War Museum, Duxford, Cambridgeshire, along with an example of the Blue Steel missile
XL318	B2	Bomber Command Hall, RAF Museum, Hendon, Greater London
XL319	B2	North East Aircraft Museum, Usworth, Northumberland
XL360	B2	Midland Air Museum, Coventry, Warwickshire
XL426/G-VJET	B2	Vulcan Restoration Trust, Southend, Essex

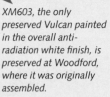

XM603, the only preserved Vulcan painted in the overall anti-radiation white finish, is preserved at Woodford, where it was originally assembled.

The Bomber Hall at the RAF Museum, Hendon, houses XL318, which is displayed with 1,000lb 'iron' bombs.

The Midland Air Museum's B2 XL360.
(Kev Storer)

VRT's Vulcan B2 XL426 making a fast taxi run at Southend.
(Richard Clarkson VRT)

655 Maintenance and Preservation Society's XM655 is in taxiable condition at Wellesbourne Mountford.

Vulcan B2 XM598 is preserved at the RAF Museum, Cosford.

The IWM has Vulcan B2 XJ824 in its collection at Duxford.

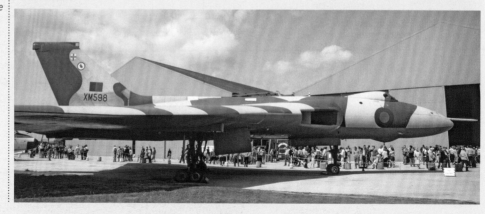

XM575/G-BLMC B2	East Midlands Airport Aeropark, Leicestershire
XM594	B2	Newark Air Museum, Winthorpe, Notts
XM597	B2	Royal Scottish Museum of Flight, East Fortune, Lothian
XM598	B2	RAF Museum, Cosford, Shropshire
XM603	B2	Avro Aircraft Heritage Society, Woodford, Greater Manchester
XM607	B2	Gate guardian at RAF Waddington, Lincolnshire
XM612	B2	City of Norwich Aviation Museum, Norwich, Norfolk
XM655/G-VULC B2	The 655 Maintenance and Preservation Society, Wellesbourne Mountford, Warwickshire

PRESERVED OVERSEAS

XL361 B2   Goose Bay AFB, Labrador, Canada

XM573 B2   SAC Museum, Offutt Air Force Base, Nebraska, USA

XM605 B2   Castle Air Museum, Atwater, California, USA

XM606 B2   Barksdale Air Force Base, Bossier City, Louisiana, USA

PRESERVED NOSE/COCKPIT SECTIONS

XH527 B2 (MRR)   Bournemouth Aviation Museum

XH560 K2   Privately owned, Foulness

XH563 B2 (MRR)   Privately owned, Bruntingthorpe

XL388 B2   Aeroventure, Doncaster

XL445 K2   Norfolk and Suffolk Aviation Museum, Flixton

XM569 B2   Gloucestershire Aviation Collection, stored Gloucester

XM602 B2   Avro Aircraft Heritage Society/Vulcan to the Sky Trust, Bruntingthorpe

XM652 B2   Privately owned, Welshpool